JUST THOUGHTS
Intuitive Connections

THOMAS PASEKA

Copyright © 2023 by Thomas Paseka

ISBN: 978-1-77883-092-1 (Paperback)

All rights reserved. No part of this publication may be reproduced, distributed, or transmitted in any form or by any means, including photocopying, recording, or other electronic or mechanical methods, without the prior written permission of the publisher, except in the case brief quotations embodied in critical reviews and other noncommercial uses permitted by copyright law.

The views expressed in this book are solely those of the author and do not necessarily reflect the views of the publisher, and the publisher hereby disclaims any responsibility for them. Some names and identifying details in this book have been changed to protect the privacy of individuals.

BookSide Press
877-741-8091
www.booksidepress.com
orders@booksidepress.com

Welcome family, friends, and those just passing by, Having noticed the fast pace we are moving, are you wondering if it is weighing on us? My sense of it is yes! Now I am starting to take time and really pick up my priorities. Being simple, I am just turning more of "the mechanics of man" off and enjoying the sounds of everyday life. The kids sounds in my background, the wind blowing as I feel a sense of fall already, even though hot out. That is what is bringing in the calm. I feel what my higher intelligence is making known. Take in the peace and silence of the natural elements as they speak, and you are to be amazed.

Thomas Paseka

Dedicated to

Ric (Reginald) Custer

Thomas Paseka

All we need is in front of us.
In the complexities of seeking,
the simplistic opens the window of opportunity
to understand that which gives us peace,

Allowing the ultimate energy of consciousness
to show us that random acts of kindness
are keys that propel us forward
in understanding of life situations.

Witnessing changes brings awareness,
then the insight's bigger shift.
The results can be phenomenal when engaged.

Introspection: the power of self.
How riveting are self reflections?
Insights ricochet from facet to facet,
until returned to the center of all understanding.
Infinite intelligence.

Ego is the defense mechanism employed when lacking insights to understand truth.

Playing safe,
like a reprieve,
chance to relax,
to catch the breath.
Energy moves forward.
A glimpse allows the move,
by just being aware.

Thomas Paseka

Learn not to fear or resist
the inevitable discomfort
that is experienced when
processing emotions.
It is through experience one grows.

We tame our reactions to life
by embracing and reflecting,
until we come to acceptance of what is,
which then eliminates
the chaos and drama in life.

Thomas Paseka

Agitation: distraction from the living God.

Ego crisis,
when one realizes
the conscious mind
is the beginning and ending
of all that is.

Thomas Paseka

Vibrational consciousness is different.
Like vibration connections create.
Anything is possible.
Different vibrations in one's path
are intuitively sensed.
Interpretation or course of action
at moment needs not always
be understood.
Just file in your memories til needed.

Just Thoughts—Intuitive Connections

Inner beliefs become our outer world.

Thomas Paseka

Present moment awareness
is eternal consciousness.
When shared, it radiates forever.

The beauty of failure is rebirth, a clean slate.

Thomas Paseka

Just to sit
allows silence to calm one,
so peace can enter,
to soothe the soul.

Just Thoughts—Intuitive Connections

You cannot keep
hurting a person you love,
and expect them
to keep liking you.

Thomas Paseka

The heart always speaks under the words.

When people walk away from you,
let them go.
Your destiny is not tied
to anyone.
Just because some leave,
does not mean they are bad.
It just means
their part in your story
is over.

Thomas Paseka

Present moment is not a destination.
It is an infinite items journey.

Living responsibly is not being a victim or victor.

Thomas Paseka

As one walks the trail of life,
sobering experiences awaken
those seeking consciousness.

What we fight are keys to our awakening.

Thomas Paseka

Do not be upset.
Things do get better.
It may be stormy now,
but it cannot rain forever.

All of life is an expression,
the essence which is love.

Thomas Paseka

One does not usually
allow enough time
to know the higher self.

Obedience to truth neutralizes corruption.

Thomas Paseka

I am not broken.
I am just fine-tuning my glitches.

If I do not feel what I see, how can I share?

Thomas Paseka

Until a soul feels its worth
as a child of the universe,
how can one know,
the essence of life is love.

Breathe in joy and strength.
Breathe out wisdom and peace.

Thomas Paseka

In the moment of seeming defeat,
ready to quit your pursuit,
usually is just before a miracle happens.
Do not cave in.
Rely on the universe once more.

Peace is a continuous act of loving the world.

Thomas Paseka

Until we balance our soul,
events do not change.
Demonstrations are changing situations,
becoming more intense,
demanding and felt,
until the soul integrates truth.

Cognitive dissonance:
a feeling of discomfort
when holding two or more conflicting
ideas, beliefs and values.
Holding on to these aspects
are reactions used to escape discomfort
from the chaos of inner conflict.

Thomas Paseka

Consciousness through
subconscious revelations
humbles.
Then may one begin to realize
the force from within,
Love.

I know a lot, but do I understand?

Thomas Paseka

One cannot extract
from another
anything that one has not
removed from themselves.

When facing life,
ask what it is teaching you,
not what it is taking from you.

Thomas Paseka

Everyone is a reflection.
Reflections are insights
to the whys of how one reacts
to experiences we have.

As long as the mind believes
what it was taught to be good
without questioning,
it can be a deficit to our
joy and peace,
as it may not be truth.

Thomas Paseka

The effects that cause spiritual pain
are one's shadows, the unfelt.

Mankind is the ground floor
for the coalescence
of the conscious and unconscious
into a unified field.

Thomas Paseka

Surrendering the mind
to infinite intelligence
creates a pathway
to the limits of the intellect,
through which one can remove
the clutter of the mind.

Look through your heart, not your eyes.
One is to be in awe as to what can be seen.
Allow, allow, allow.

Thomas Paseka

If disappointment has shattered a dream
do not let your light go out.
Live it up at the bottom.
There is a new treasure, one's peace of mind.

I know I am,
as I know we are,
one in purpose,
Love.

Thomas Paseka

In the moment, all answers are possible.

Consciousness through subconscious revelation humbles.
When one begins to realize the force within, love, peace is an achievable reality.

Thomas Paseka

Embracing experiences,
instead of resistance,
is the gateway to integrating
all the chaos in life.

Thomas Paseka, Intuitive reader
Contact: dayfrank2@gmail.com

www.ingramcontent.com/pod-product-compliance
Ingram Content Group UK Ltd.
Pitfield, Milton Keynes, MK11 3LW, UK
UKHW020244240426
12048UKWH00026B/1600